TELL THIS TO THE UNIVERSE

YESYES BOOKS | PORTLAND

THE UNIVERSE

KATIE PRINCE

TELL THIS TO THE UNIVERSE © 2024 BY KATIE PRINCE

COVER & INTERIOR DESIGN: ALBAN FISCHER
COVER ART: "THE OPENING," © 2021 BY ALEAH CHAPIN
PROJECT LEAD: KMA SULLIVAN
PHOTO CREDIT: GABRIEL MOSELEY

ISBN 978-1-936919-98-7
PRINTED IN THE UNITED STATES OF AMERICA

PUBLISHED BY YESYES BOOKS
1631 NE BROADWAY ST #121
PORTLAND, OR 97232
YESYESBOOKS.COM

KMA SULLIVAN, PUBLISHER
DEVIN DEVINE, ASSISTANT EDITOR
ALBAN FISCHER, GRAPHIC DESIGNER
KARAH KEMMERLY, MANAGING EDITOR
JILL KOLONGOWSKI, MANUSCRIPT COPY EDITOR
JAMES SULLIVAN, ASSISTANT EDITOR
GALE MARIE THOMPSON, SENIOR EDITOR, BOOK DEVELOPMENT

for everyone I've lost

CONTENTS

dark matter ✴ 1

i.
poem in which I am leaning against a car ✴ 5
a thousand untouched islands ✴ 6
"astronomers capture violent newborn star" ✴ 7
you feel like a city I could know ✴ 9
imagine a world in which there is nothing ✴ 10
Forrest, dead at twenty-five ✴ 11
upon hearing he has been cremated ✴ 12
the body as a collection of spinning particles ✴ 14
feeling ill in a novelty restaurant ✴ 15
gridlocked, I-95 ✴ 16
when the *mara* weights my chest I see ✴ 17

ii.
there is a world in which soup doesn't film ✴ 21
Askja ✴ 22
when you asked what makes me happy ✴ 24
this mimicked dance ✴ 26
drinking on the porch with a fellow recluse ✴ 27
theories of relativity ✴ 28
there is a thief in me ✴ 29
poem in which the sun is a balding and jealous lover ✴ 31
we call man an insect infinite ✴ 33
a secret ✴ 36
the moral of the story is *bears aren't friends* ✴ 37
poem in which acid rain is just acid ✴ 39

iii.

in memoriam: I will build you a body of words, I will ✳ 43
poem in which I drive drunk ✳ 49
here the clocks tick endlessly to nowhere ✳ 50

iv.

armistice ✳ 53
a winter story ✳ 54
no vacancy ✳ 56
escapism as a quantum thought experiment ✳ 58
family reunion (or, the Norsemen return) ✳ 59
language in which *slabb* is the worst kind of snow ✳ 60
there is a world in which you must wear a coat of cold ✳ 62
what is a forest if not every loud thing echoed ✳ 63
grief as art appreciation ✳ 64
poem in which I am trapped in a thousand snowy valleys ✳ 65

v.

what is a traveler if not every strange thing ✳ 69
I wake in an old factory ✳ 70
if I were a speeding train (a cyborg love song) ✳ 71
o hell o hell that mild thing ✳ 72
what this lacks is understanding ✳ 73
on escaping black holes ✳ 75
a few things that haunt me ✳ 77
here the clouds are wool blankets ✳ 78
lambda means god if you're searching for one ✳ 80
terraform ✳ 81
poem in which I am driving toward a home ✳ 87

NOTES ✳ 89
ACKNOWLEDGMENTS ✳ 93

TELL THIS TO THE UNIVERSE

DARK MATTER

a version of me exists   in nine time zones.   I wind clocks in twenty countries. and always the setting sun   and always the rising dark.   and always the thought of you,   usually as a man. sometimes a bear or glacier or black black ocean.

      to exist inside a shell,   see the sound of waves or   a bright flash of sky.   when I was young my uncle bought explosives,   worked fire into shapes in the backyard night.
                        and my grandmother died.

   and my mother a fallen apart thing, a bird with onionskin wings.   in Australia I climbed   a mountain. a sunrise lit the canopy and the world   was built with feathers.   and always the thought of you   of what I can't see.

here is a dark matter.   I don't know how to reach you, and   wondering takes up   all my time. the rolled-back clocks and the close.   this empty bed. last night   I dreamt my mother died.   my brother coughed up his lungs   in the next room,
      left some bloody mess on bluish walls.

a beast clawed a message   in the ice
on the sill.   it says *cake wrists*
in mud, stick feathers in.   step off or fly.
my brother is a long shadow cast
            across oceans, an uncertain god
hunched over a small spun-out   earth.

I am always in the dark, here.   there is
a whole universe to lose.
you planetary mist   you earthless dust.
is there a word
            for the weight of empty space?
is it *here* or *drift* or *leave* or *lost* ?

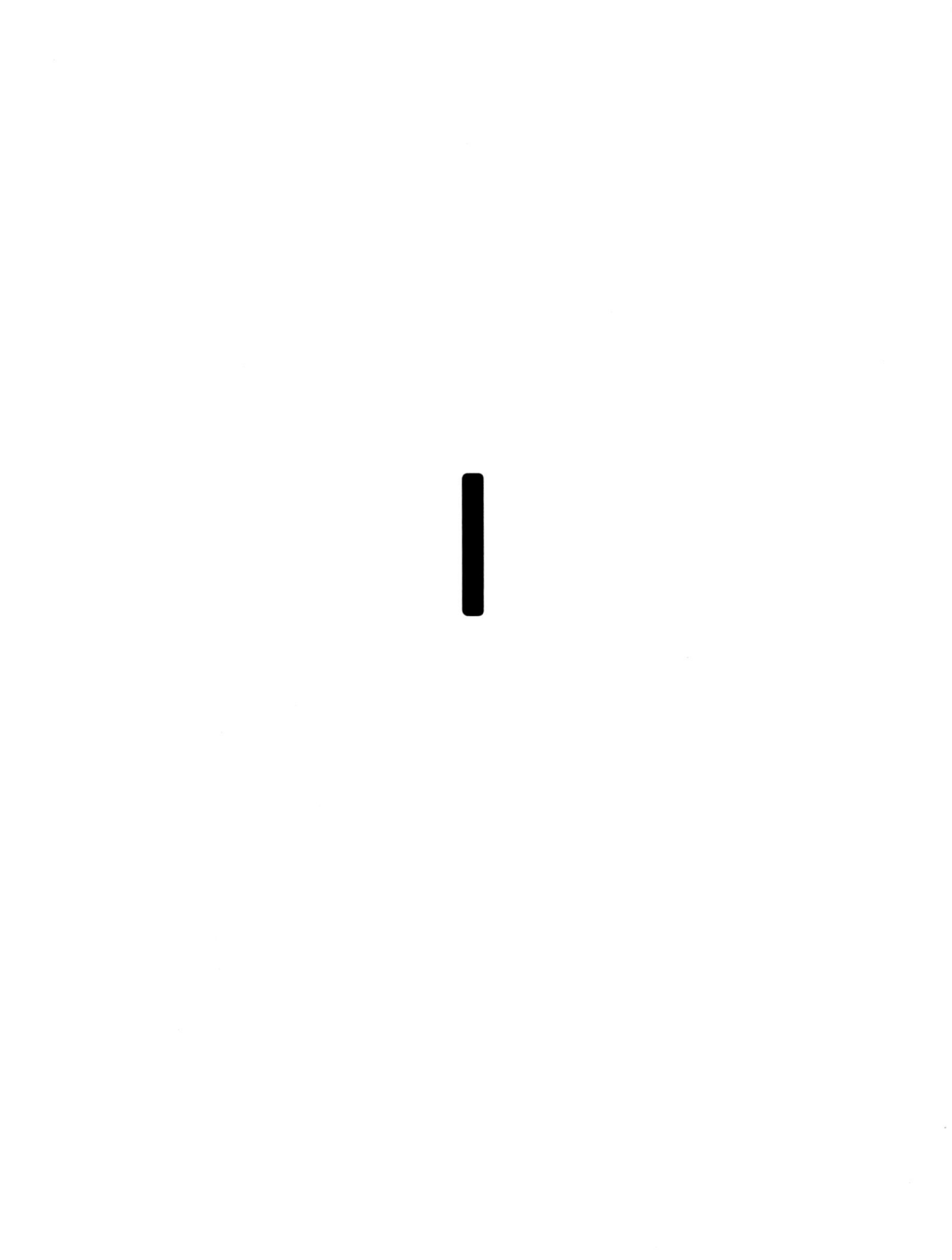

POEM IN WHICH I AM LEANING AGAINST A CAR

& watching a lightning storm. in which I am a thing
needing to be struck. how each bolt turns the night to day—

above all, I wish to be a lit current. I left one place & long
to leave it all again. the eastern ocean a mirror west.

ever the next horizon, and the next—what name
is there for this hollowness? the midnight drift

inside my chest. I am filled with untruths:
a unicorn hoof in place of a heart, pillows

in place of lungs. when I breathe I choke on the soft of me.
each time thunder cracks my body contracts, folds

against itself like a lightless paper lantern. I want
to be able to speak about things outside my skin.

when lightning strikes I close my eyes & I am
elsewhere: a galaxy with no sign of life

where the sun is white & intermittent
& there's always a loud noise to follow—

A THOUSAND UNTOUCHED ISLANDS

St. Lawrence River, Redwood, New York

today I saw Canada across the water, ached
to touch it but it felt like a dream
upon waking—all intangible fog

and quiet. I am all sinew, no bone: a tight
uneven heat connecting nothing. when I stretch

I feel my atoms separate. their escape

a prickle of light. I burn holes through your clothes
while you work. what fills this three feet
between my chest and yours if not some white-hot

need? I am nothing but my want.

picture an untouched body—call it
this bleeding clatter of bone
and muscle, this river I can't cross.

I think the sun must be scorching Canada's skin
today, but here—standing on this granite riverbed,
ankles paling in the wet—here

there is nothing but wind and I am looking in

and I am breathless and I know my body
exists—this pair of salt-raw and opened lips

"ASTRONOMERS CAPTURE VIOLENT NEWBORN STAR"

think *the womb of space*, or *empty
pockets, their lint*. some millions

of years between, & this just
a light show—do you see?
the butterfly net cast across

galaxies—asteroids & comets
slipping unseen through the mesh

& isn't it such a mystery—the looking
back in time, the wrapping of the mind
around the word *distant*

the fact is, it's all so much farther

than we realize. these days I find myself
mired in science. at night my blinds
cast shadows across angled walls,

supernovae teased from flashing blue
police beacons below. I lie next to you

or no one & it is almost a comfort
to know that we are made of quarks
that we are as much carbon as dying

stars & what I mean is, we're all so
much farther than we feel, touching

but not touching in the afterglow
of a violent beginning—the purple-red
spread of all this universal burning

YOU FEEL LIKE A CITY I COULD KNOW

your stone-faced buildings, your bodegas.
your next-door delis. I want to lay my hands
against all your glass, let it absorb me like it does

the sun's heat. you summer sweat, you too many
citizens' sweltering breaths. even the garbage
wants something. my body thinks it knows

you from some faraway dream, one I've had
and forgotten a thousand red-eyed times, of a lover

I hardly knew, who lives in my mind as heavy arms
and a desperate silent need to be held. the train
rocks me to sleep aside another hundred passengers.

in a city like you, no one stands out. a city like you
is a wash of high expectations. you dirty streets. you
rush. you keep blocking the sun, I keep wanting in.

IMAGINE A WORLD IN WHICH THERE IS NOTHING

but a large gasping breath
in which first you are outside
and then you are in and you
don't know where or whose
body this is but it is dark and
it is wet and it smells fetid like
the spreading start of infection
and you wonder if this means
you will come hurtling back out
yours is just a violent existence
a hacking end or beginning
maybe call this the big bang
or the big thump on the chest
the big mucus-covered start
of all of it you bacteria you
disease you lonely small thing

FORREST, DEAD AT TWENTY-FIVE

there's no such thing as sorry enough—or sorry
at all—when you think about it. there's no such thing
as knowing what someone else needs or wants
or could do for you if you let them. I once nursed a bird
on the verge of death and when it was strong enough
it bit my hand and flew away, and I was crushed,
but I had done what it needed, could do nothing more. I wanted
to matter but in the end just knowing a life is there
because you cared must be enough to feel worthy, or feel
something like hope. sometimes I'm sure I've known
this shock, this nausea, this horror before—but maybe
it was in a book that I saw the boy strap fireworks
to the cat, watched it run across the field
terrified by the heat against its back. Forrest
used to light bottle rockets with cigarettes and hold them
in his hands until they exploded, singed his skin. he would tell me
it was better to feel than to wish you did. I would wrap his hands
with neosporin and bandages and try to make it go away
but I couldn't fix his burnt fingers, much less
all the things that smoldered underneath. at the time
we were teenagers. at the time, we were cruel to everyone
but each other. sometimes it kills me, the ways we'll never grow up,
the way I was always the one who let us fall out of touch. sometimes
I wonder who hurt him that much. sometimes I wish
I could make them sorry enough.

UPON HEARING HE HAS BEEN CREMATED

i.
some nights when I am standing in my bedroom staring at the wall it occurs to me that I have done this a million times. I should stare at something that will shift into another thing. sometimes I drink just to watch colors change, to fool myself, to pretend I see more than your silhouette in the way the ash settles as the incense burns. I've never seen you for what you are. to me, you are misspelled words, you are helvetica in a gray speech bubble, you are so god damn boring and far away. these days I dream in helvetica. everything about you is wrong and yet here I am, staring at the wall until the colors in the photos change into letters, into what I know of you.

ii.
I don't want I don't I will not. I will write his name until it is no longer a name, until it is shapes that don't make sense together, or loss, or the way things disappear when you look at them too long. it is me spending too much time looking at nothing, willing it to be something. it is last week when she said, *I didn't want you to hear it from someone else,* and I thought, I didn't want to hear it from you I didn't want to hear it at all. I think I will stop hearing and maybe then I'll finally see things again that aren't your name, or his, or the way his mother must have looked when she found him that day.

iii.
there is an ocean nearby that I never see. there is a word on my tongue that I'll never use. there is a name that doesn't belong to him, that is waiting to be claimed. we are all just sitting still and looking out the window wondering where people really go when they die, if they go anywhere at all.

iv.

here is the house your father built. now this heap of ash. you say *accident* but it wasn't, and I want to say *I know* but I don't. I want, though, to burn something to the ground, to feel the power of knowing I've set something uncontrollable in motion, something that won't stop consuming until there isn't anything left. it is what and when and how we are, consuming each other until we are both empty and quiet and done, filled with dense smoke and the ruin of ash. maybe when it's all burnt down we can move on to something smoother, cooler, wetter—or maybe just deader, like him. sometimes I think if we keep on this way we'll both end up like him.

THE BODY AS A COLLECTION OF SPINNING PARTICLES

if you had no nucleus
    would you call yourself composed
        could you track the spin

of all your moving parts
    would you try to stitch your skin together
        if it ached to be apart

FEELING ILL IN A NOVELTY RESTAURANT

the scene: yellow walls and too much eye contact.
an uncertainty nobody feels or nobody wants to.
betty boop winks from the wall. the word *hate*
doesn't fit the tone but gets said anyway.
all this wide-eyed uncomfortable silence,
all this white noise. a beer gone. a struck-out stack
of stale chips. some mild salsa. this stone broke
feast. this trash on the floor. all the directionless
anger neither needs express. both a skipping
record, *I don't know why I do things like this.*
this cold, wet taco. a wilted shred of brown
lettuce. the bitter thick of breath. neither needs
to sit in this booth tonight. nobody is willing to leave.

GRIDLOCKED, I-95

brake lights. break—something constructed,
this collapse of cars, stopped, a rubber streak
of street. the road at night should stretch

like the sky can't, should end in haze
& soft black sheets. a dream: my car on fire,
a stranger's baby born in the backseat.

the fog of sickness. I am floating above
the glacier of you—my chest rubbed mint-raw,
a frozen breath clearing. I want

to punctuate these sentences so there is more
silence. call me an unlit highway, a traffic cone
overturned, the accident we're all slowing down

to watch. there are so many things none of us
remember how to say, or do. what does it mean
to feel unstuck? I am hinged to a wall,

a shut door, a close orbit. I have never
moved fluidly. the body a fit
and start. I am tired of all this talking.

WHEN THE *MARA* WEIGHTS MY CHEST I SEE

a blank ballroom an antlered beast a xylophone lacking keys and didn't you say once if you were an instrument that's what you would be? look: it's you and me, dancing. you and me in this room with its antlered beasts on the walls and red velvet like crushed blood or something broken, a bone or my spleen

or alternatively we could say a romantic comedy in which I am clumsy and fall a lot and you are suave and in love with your job and I with you from afar and I work too much and dream too little or alternatively we could say real life and it is imperfect. and you and me dancing and an altered beast falling

and we are standing in the wind-bleached bones of a rib cage mine or yours or your ex's or mine or god's or where are the words I need do you keep them with you

here in this cage and the floor against my toes is wet and spongy-cold like freezer-burnt steaks the floor is red as blood and crushed antler velvet and I am dancing and there is a xylophone intact but are you not here us a thing disappeared and this my spleen are we dreaming again no we are all

falling again. altered beasts and nothing, an altar of beasts and the hazy red-black of foreign hands pressing against my eyes, when I wish I could sleep but there is nothing but blood in me

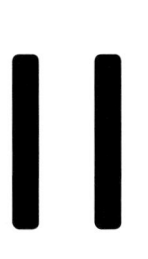

THERE IS A WORLD IN WHICH SOUP DOESN'T FILM

when it chills. in fact, there is a world
in which soup never gets cold and
contains exactly the right amount
of seasoning. there is never any left
to pour down the drain because this
is a world in which everyone is hungry
and then we are fed, in which dogs
don't feel pain when they die and nobody
dreams about running away. according
to my physics it is approximately nine
hundred seventy-eight trillion imaginary
light-years away, or six inches to the left
in innumerable parallel universes. here
there is no such thing as tomorrow, or
home, or belonging. in this world
no one has friends because no one speaks
a language. there are no misunderstandings
because no one understands a thing. here
there are no endings. there's no word for begin.

ASKJA

say it is 1967—& here is my mother
fourteen in Iowa, not knowing or caring

about the cavalcade of American astronauts
who squint in Iceland—who picture the moon
at their feet—who settle heavy bootprints into the skin

of the country my mother will never really consider
part of her (not its fish, its farms,

not our rumbling dark)—in 1967 she still watches
for sun. by this time the land is barren underfoot,

a stone-swept crater—blood rocks, maybe,
my ancestors' igneous debt.
in nearly fifty years it will look the same

but she will not & she will not
know why. imagine—all the mess inside

the earth, burst forth in violence—now
hardened gray across its face. & she will not
see anything but ice. in nearly fifty years

I will follow her & every other relative. I will fall victim
to myself on a stark autumn night—I will lose

my mind in space I will reach
for some kind of tether to tie me to earth

I will search every night for something to touch
with a telescope—& when I land on Askja
I will know I am not the first

but the volcano it rises violent in me

& it will be over in seconds—& I will finally know—

this is what it takes to feel unalone:
this surface tension, this heat. this new solid earth
& the empty beneath.

WHEN YOU ASKED WHAT MAKES ME HAPPY

I thought about leaving. is there a nice way to say I am
only happy in transit?
I will never be your destination. midair I feel lawless

my body an expanse
of possibility. is there a way to explain—when I look
out the window of the plane

I know I never want to touch
the ground again. when you told me *I want to keep seeing you*
I wanted to say *your skin is a cage. stop*

trying to trap me in your cells. instead
I said *I'm sorry* and left. I didn't know how to tell you—
I wanted the subway to last forever

I could describe how I pictured taking the blue all the way
to wonderland, how in my dreams I never
made myself arrive. I could say, when a plane takes off it becomes

a universe. would you understand why it matters
if I asked you—is there a word for the way clouds only seem solid
when they're reflecting the sunlight

or for the moonsilver hollow feel of waking
after a night spent dreaming you could fly? up here the earth
looks like nothing I need. I need you

to know I will never be happy unless I am
in motion. that loneliness
is a disease of stillness. that happy hinges on *if*—

THIS MIMICKED DANCE

I tried to make a home underwater but hours passed
& it was just a darkness & I was nothing but wet
nothing but breathless. a pruned lack

of self. what I need: a new pair of hands,
soft effortless ones that can follow the beat
you set. picture yourself an unlatched suitcase,

a trampled & unstylish hat. as yet a thing unmade.
this is how it feels to miss something. look, I don't know
how to talk to you. I think I can't get far enough away.

a fact: the fastest manmade object travels
at ninety miles per second. what this means: you could spin
me into space, send me twirling along an asteroid belt

& it would still take me five thousand lifetimes
to reach a planet that felt like home.

DRINKING ON THE PORCH WITH A FELLOW RECLUSE
after Li Po

we drink as dusk shrinks to dark. the bushes buzz,
mosquitos hum. azalea blossoms to the right, fallen
and trampled by wildlife: squirrels, a small dog.
we laugh, lights blur. skeletons sway in the breeze.
I fall into thought, wander off. you don't even hear me leave.

THEORIES OF RELATIVITY

take the statement *time is relative* & break it
into parts. this moment—you've been here before. it's a first
for me. think of it this way: time moves faster when you're closer

to earth, & I've spent so much of my life off the ground. & did you know
the universe curves around itself? this is to say we'll never touch
its ends. instead I make tiny telescopes with my hands, stare straight

into the sun & remind myself that my attraction to you is nothing
more than gravity—your mass warps everything

in my universe, wraps the light around itself so I can't be sure
what's real. either you are or you aren't. does it matter
which? I still see you in each empty space—

the reflection of sky in motor oil, the cloud of dust
kicked up by the truck that passed me on the street just now.
you are mars through a telescope. you bright & deadly thing.

THERE IS A THIEF IN ME

it is hard enough already
to take what's yours. I am

thinking of daffodils,
how if I owned a meadow
it would have none.

just that soft Irish grass.
I would install my own peat
bog to veil this lava skin.

mine the field where transparent
flowers grow. look, I will hide

you in my smallish places.
make a home behind

my knees. I take the words
we need, the voice and wind.
I echo in the fjord's edged cliffs.

I'm not asking you to steal
for me, that lawnmower
that knee brace that book

on foreign law. I am not
saying give me all the blue

you find. but if you wanted
I would hide that too.

POEM IN WHICH THE SUN IS A BALDING AND JEALOUS LOVER

let's say a sun spot is a bald spot is a burnt missing
is the sun pulling its heat out in frustration

let's say global warming is partly because
the sun is portly and losing its hair

or because it's ashamed to be smaller
than some other, more effective suns

all the other suns are much better lovers

the sun is either too hot or too cold
or too emotionally distant

and the earth is so desperate in love

she tells the sun *honey I'm holding on
to your heat*

meanwhile the sun disapproves
of the way earth dresses herself

(such shrinking foliage, such greenhouse gas)

and the way she's sending out so many satellites
trying to talk to so many other planets

and allowing so much of herself
to leave her atmosphere and allowing
so many meteorites to enter

earth says *you're smothering me why
don't you just leave*

the sun says *baby you can't exist without me*

WE CALL MAN AN INSECT INFINITE

there are motions
we have no words for—truly
no one said *we needed this—this*
is to say harm, or nostalgia
or all the ugly words for what we are
more or *less than*. a rib
or a cock or a drink in hand. upon sad
deflating breast. listen,
in the world outside I am in lust
with so many uncut
wrists—or, let's say, the oxidized
unseen back half of a face. we call man
a scabbed and seeping mess.

what I mean to say is, a bone
fragment came loose
from my skull and landed
on my tongue today, felt hard
but smooth like cut
glass. rounded, I think, against an excess
of blood flow. say *but I have no blood*
left in me. say *in space I boiled*
under, through skin: sweat
sex and plasma in a void.
I can taste the hole I left

with my tongue. say *it leads*
to the brain, say *bugs*
are crawling in or out or down.

when it's warm at night I dream
about earwigs burrowing
into soft tissue—then wake
and spit small bodies in a tin.
let's call it what it is, somebody
says. *alien implantation.*
or—a rejected host. for isn't this
the briny taste of man? of my own
brain? call it somehow short of human

or somehow far, what happens
to a body loose in space—first
boiled, then clotted
then expanded, frozen, and swept
away. to cross uncounted
miles. and here I am a year
from leaving. what I mean is from
breaking out. what I mean is *a face
bloated with fluids*—but
will the head still swell
if the mouth is full of holes?

I excavate myself with a foreign
tongue. listen. I slid the bone
fragment against the edge
of my desk, laid it down to
decompose. I am afraid to dispose
of my skull. we might call this
molting, or building
a new self out of unusable
parts. say *I am a woman playing
with her own stones.* say *I am
searching* for Space A

in which to place Bone B.
look, this is nothing unforeseen.
we call man a broken
down machine.

A SECRET

    I have never felt like exactly what I am

I have been a desert, a swamp, a metal box
    on wheels, a balloon burst or burned
        I have been a building bruised and blessed

THE MORAL OF THE STORY IS
BEARS AREN'T FRIENDS

i.

they called her *cautionary tale*. it isn't the prettiest name but she wasn't the prettiest girl. she walked to the shore and pulled a bear from the water, said *you don't belong*—he interrupted, said *roar*, something to that effect. she thought he meant *here*, meant *neither do you*. meant, *we are the same*. we all know bears don't talk but sometimes we make words out of sounds, see meaning where it isn't. when he bit off her arm she was surprised that it didn't hurt, that arms can float like logs or alligators or inner tubes. as it bobbed away she pictured it as a raft for a small rodent lost at sea. more likely, it was food for fish or sharks or small rodents lost at sea.

ii.

the bear had been lounging when an unremarkable girl came and yanked him out of the water. he gave her a little help because she strained and her fingers knotted his fur and it hurt, and it was clear she wasn't going to stop trying to move him until she did. he roared to scare her and she smiled vacantly like she was stoned and thought she was watching a movie or making a friend or living in a fairy tale. he was tired of them thinking he was cuddly, some happy helper animal who cared about people and their problems. it wasn't his fault his fur was so soft and his belly so round. it wasn't his fault so he bit off her arm. he bit off her arm and she blinked, smiled vacantly.

iii.

you know a one-armed girl will never find a husband. she could hear her mother saying it, her stepmother saying it, her grandmother saying it, all these versions of mother with lips equally red and equally thin, all their mouths overflowing with the same bad-tasting geriatric words. she didn't much care. she liked the bear. liked the way her blood looked spreading through the water, a breadcrumb trail that led to her lost arm. she used her other arm to hug the bear and he ripped it off with his claws. she leaned her torso against him and buried her face in his fur until he toppled backward into the water. his fur was so soft, his belly so round. she thought *a raft, an adventure, a friend to guide me.* she thought *who needs a husband.*

iv.

the bear was perturbed by the now-armless girl that flopped against him. she looked like a doll, the kind that might attract serial killers and perverts but little girls would never buy in the store. *nobody wants a no-armed girl* he thought. he didn't even want to eat her. he rolled her body off his own and she splashed into the water. he lumbered away, sought a quieter stretch of shore. her body bobbed in the waves, soggy with blood, with salt. when he had gone twenty feet he turned and she was ten feet closer to China, head bobbing like an apple. a hedgehog had staked claim on her body, planted a flag in her bellybutton. it curled between her breasts like a conquistador after a long day of devastation. the bear watched, feeling lazy. the girl floated. smiled vacantly.

POEM IN WHICH ACID RAIN IS JUST ACID

Or, poem in which most people die. Nobody is sad about it. In a swampy poem it mists all the time. The rain eats through steel bridges and signs, warps cars into piles of melted engine. The boats sink at their docks and all the fish float belly-up, no eyes in their sockets. All the homes are moldy skeletons, cracked foundations lacking insulation and walls. Everywhere is a streak of stripped paint is driftwood is a hurricane's aftermath. In this poem, no one is allowed outdoors without a reinforced black umbrella. Hospitals are filled with scared faces peeling off in sheets, people who are now equal amounts visible bone and melted skin. *I used to love to dance in the rain* they'll say through their misshapen not-mouths, their shiny pink skin grafts. Nobody laughs out loud then goes home and cries about it. Nobody sits in the dark with an umbrella while rain burns through the roof. Nobody asks where we will go when the rain eats away the floor. Everyone says *we did this to ourselves, there has never been such thing as an accident.* Everyone is certain about these things. Nobody knows not to touch the rain. Nobody will leave this poem whole.

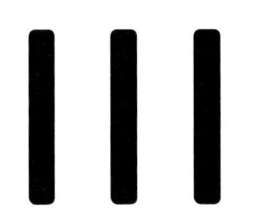

III

IN MEMORIAM: I WILL BUILD YOU A BODY OF WORDS, I WILL

i. There is a world in which the big dipper is the freckles on my arm

It is in some other universe Which is named this human body

Call me a benevolent god if you want I will run this place

into the ground The brain is the faulty cog in this machine

It is the reason no one ever speaks You a speck on planet

skin cell six thousand thirteen Me in an unlit office wishing

to be dust in a multiverse To have another irrelevant god

in orbit near me Right now you are a part of this system but

some sweaty night you will disappear in a washing machine

All your mountains and prairies will sink Your citizens will

drown in something sudsy and clean This is a universe in which

Chris is still alive In which he drove into a field of cattle instead

of a lake In which his seizure stopped his car was fine he slept

until he woke and everything mooed all around him This is

a universe in which we are all leaving each other all the time

but mostly it is one in which no one dies until I let them

ii. poem in which I drive straight into a lightning storm

inside the storm there is nothing but wet & static / inside the storm my metal fillings taste like batteries & leave acid burns on my tongue / there are so many ways September is trying to hurt / see the rain falling in my car / picture what it might have been / a white mustang fills with stagnant water a gunmetal quiet the blur of no air / thinking stakes me / I can't breathe / a stuck fork that electrical socket / these days all I dream of are brain waves / do you see me drawing activity on the EEG / everything I know how to say is wrong / I say *you are part of the earth* & I stab a shovel in it scrape out its insides until I get to the magma underneath / I say *you were not in your body anymore anyway* & I don't know where to look / & you have no mouth left to tell me / I say *energy can neither be created nor destroyed* & I rip the universe at its seams to find you

iii. how to go home

begin by passing Houston. see a boxed giant,
an endless sprawl. try lifting its buildings from the dirt.

now, set them farther apart. a person is a place
is a monolithic ending. or: a microscopic meteorite. an intersection, a collision
all the weight of earth and sky. you are too close

to home today. your denial won't survive in the sunlight. see it bleach
your eyes. see the way bodies become cities

become collections of bones and trash and buildings.
from far away your figure will fill with
the empty flat of Texas—the treeless brown, the slack wind. you will yell

from the wasteland of your chest, you will say *but I have been in love*
with so many landscapes. if you could you would build all of them into monuments

you would put them inside yourself and keep them safe
you would give them the names of past lovers, all the men you miss
and don't. your body is a desert at night

but it is made of salt. pretend not to feel the skyscrapers
you are constructing in your rib cage, pretend those towers

of loss do not scratch the sides of your throat. ask—if a place is a person
what happens when Dallas is here
but Chris is not? you will say, *Dallas is standing air is dirt*

is heat is lacking half its self. and no time to build him a home
inside you. and this a statue half finished.

iv. elegy for all the times we used to get drunk

in the church where his memorial service
is being held. a game of marked cards jenga a falling block

& no one ever won but we were never done arguing—

say, *who is better at this game,* or *if there are twenty-eight crosses
in this room does that mean god can see us touching*

one summer the rain wouldn't stop & his windshield wipers
were not fast enough to clear the water & the parking lots

outside were a bluish blur & we laid in the back soaked
& wrapped up in ourselves & it was the first time

I saw a car as an island, or a home—us

buzzed in the mustang because we never wanted to live
anywhere else. a Texas September is a window down, & I can't close

my eyes without wondering how it felt. if he saw it
coming. in the past we were always underwater—now I am

outside I am touching his name it is sunny & dry & I am talking
to the ashes I am saying—*remember how we never knew how to change*

how Texas felt like a flood & I loved you once

v. safe travels

Your body swells within
itself   It presses
close against your skin & bones
This plane can't
take off fast enough it can't take
off   You come
home & never want to leave   You
don't know who
home is   You are lounging on a wing
looking to be
blown off   In your ear a woman
sings *safe travels*
don't die but he did & you know
sad is a creeping
disease   an interior bloat
Think his brain
think the accident think burning
a body until
the water that killed it turns
to steam   Your body
swells into an ocean of salt & bile
& everything seeping
out the skin   & you never knew grief
would taste
so rancid   like a bloodied animal
so many years
dead   So long unburied

vi. there is a tear in the universe, it looks like a smile

the clouds look like equations tonight. water vapor plus late-afternoon light equals a godly sheen. I've never thought long about cremation but the veins turn to ash, too. the teeth. the lips and eyes. is life a wet thing? I am drifting above a gray ditch—this must be how the dead see the earth. it haze, we static. a corpse crushed beneath dirt makes a suffocating kind of sense. but ash. but youth. a first love robbed of brain & body. the pastor says there are signs all around us. flowers, trees, sunsets, rain: he calls these proof. I am looking for god but my faith lives in mathematics. would you believe it, love? all those times we got drunk in church, & none of it ever rubbed off on me.

POEM IN WHICH I DRIVE DRUNK

somebody says   *but you know*
that could kill you   somebody says *it's*
the end of the world   as I know it
and what I didn't tell my best friend:
         I drove on the wrong side
of the road   for too long a time
I didn't say   *I played chicken*
and I was drunk   like I was
in a '50s high school movie
like I was seventeen   like I knew
what I was doing   what I didn't say
was   *this is my body and I want*
to mangle it   what I didn't say was
         does it matter who dies
I didn't say   *if Chris why not*
me   I didn't say   *who wants to live*
anyway   because who wants to see
what it's like at the end   when no one
can talk about anything but
their own pain   can say
anything but   *I know that this is how*
         it feels when a body begins
to decay   what I said was   *I can't*
stand for it to be this way

HERE THE CLOCKS TICK ENDLESSLY TO NOWHERE

in Icelandic half-ten means nine-thirty. when Mark says it's half-ten he means it's ten-thirty. *klukkan er hálf tíu,* I say to nobody who understands. I stare at the numbers, they tell me nothing. the needle struggles to move but can't and I ache to help it along. the clock melts down the wall like a bad Dalí imitation. it started to smear almost *þrjú* months ago when my home burned to ash, or maybe around the time I tried to speak to my ancestors but the words came out all *th* and wisp. now when it ticks the needles sit at half-stuck. I stare daggers through the babyshit-green wall. I trace your face in the dull spackle. you're laughing but I can't remember how that sounds. it's been almost three months, though I swear you died yesterday. this could become the first night I haven't cried. *það gæti* I say to myself. the clock ticks. I watch. the needle won't budge. I don't blink. my eyes water, then spill. I say *er miðnætti.* I say *kannski á morgun.* I hold my breath. my pulse ticks in time.

IV

ARMISTICE

consider last autumn a war
and today the quiet restlessness
that follows. when the bricks must be relaid

but building comes second to sleep
and sleep comes second to wine.
certain nights we think *it will heal
itself without our help*. it's possible

we're right. better to sit and wait
for summer, sip slowly from our glasses
and shiver through the damp of February.
ignore our itching bones. we shouldn't miss

the fighting or the losing, yet
we do. these days even the wind can't decide
whether it's moving or standing still.

A WINTER STORY

look at me, at my tiny ice house. I am living
    like a queen in this smallish freeze.

the logs in my fireplace are too wet
    to catch. the ceiling drips on the crown

of my head. bow to me, the wet ice queen.
    I am something no one needs.

somebody said, *all women like you*
    are icy. all women think they are queens.

somebody's man handprint left a dent
    in the snow. it was not

    an apology but an imprint.
    I heard it land, a beating.

    felt it softly bruise. in this story
a large branch breaks into my house. a large

    branch shatters my walls
& windowsills, loses his leaves in my living

    space. and what now—I, a queen,
and no fortress in which to feel safe? I collect

slivers of house into the long train
of my gown. I nest among ruins

and remainders, build myself anew
from red-gold tears. I issue one command:

may no one ever reach me here.

NO VACANCY

I drink a flat white.   In Australia I drink
              this. In Iowa the ground is a flat
white. Wet paper, paint. I drink   white
paint. Thick   in throat. I stand
in lukewarm coffee. Or   I stand in
too-hot coffee. White melts   off my skin,
I am fragile   and pale as untainted
eggshells.

          My mother painted
          a room eggshell white, so when
we stood inside we could feel   as though
we were clean, or safe.   This world,
the bone of my inner ear. When I spill coffee
it whorls   across the tablecloth's white.
Coffee-cut rivers   through snow, or
paper.   I walk a flat white path.

          In Australia it is summer but I am
a wintered beast.   Behind my parents' house
are nine speckled deer   which
disappear as I approach. The ground a
coconut slush. I drank   from a coconut
in Fiji, in June. It was winter then,
          like now. The deer slide down an
incline white and I follow. I want to know
what they know.

                The cliffs under my white
blanket are unflat and untasted.   I am
tumbling   like Kelly did in Queensland.
I am tumbling into   a pot.
        My father makes a warm potato soup
but I am not a swimmer.   I slurp
from a bowl   of patchwork farmland. I lie
flat under a sheath   of white
water.

In Queensland I rafted   a nameless river.
The cyclone decimated   the last line
of the poem. For years   I dreamt
of crocodile tears   of my body moving
through mud slicks. Once   I dived
the Great Barrier Reef—from underwater
all the world was a flat white sun:
rippled and sharp   and shrunk.
        There was bile in my breathing tube.

            Listen, I am no ozone.
These are no vacancies.   My brother
drives a continental rift.   His spine
a metal hinge.   I stand knee-deep in clouds.
He shovels,   lifts and flings. My mother
paints him in her sleep.   We power-wash
at dawn. An eggshell wall, some thought
of loss.   Look   the words
they've been wrong   all along.

ESCAPISM AS A QUANTUM THOUGHT EXPERIMENT

sometimes the earth is the size of an atom
    & I make this house
a spaceship & you
       are there & you are gone—

FAMILY REUNION (OR, THE NORSEMEN RETURN)

how the home becomes a minefield
of blind red giants. they collect and stomp

on glasses. eat all the ducks, the geese.
the whiskey is gone. they sing
as one, then buy more. when I stand in the hall

I wage war with myself. this is to say

I pour another drink. Malibu and Sprite, so
I will be a tropical island. Iowa
crowds in on all sides. my drink is too wet.

we need more ice. we leave. tamp snow
to forge crowns. bags bought at the gas station
slung over shoulders like sons.

to glory! they say. the bluster of kings.

LANGUAGE IN WHICH *SLABB* IS THE WORST KIND OF SNOW

my cousin points to a sentence, says *try
to translate this*. I do not understand

the way the nouns decline. in my new
language there are fifty-six words

for wind, more than a hundred for snow.
as humans we are bound, noosed

by weather systems. by the indomitable
cold. in the old calendar Iceland has six

months of *vetur*. we sleep, drink *glögg*
through the dark, trudge through the *slabb*

that comes with *vor* and signals warmth.
my language is a thawing season.

at night I watch myself come unglued—molting
a former self into crackling grass. my skin

flakes into a landscape the dead-yellow
of summer, the red of desert clay. in dreams

I am haunted by *Ísland*, by gray, by lava
fields that are never as hot against my feet

as I need them to be. where the rain drives
black-eyed and sharp—an eclipse in horizontal

sheets. this, my *mara*, my slush-slick streets.
all stick, all dirt, all treacherous *is*.

THERE IS A WORLD IN WHICH YOU MUST WEAR A COAT OF COLD

if you want to survive. you might

think of it as a binding: of snow, or ice

or a rough pair of hands. we are all looking

to slough off the worst of ourselves.

in this world your coat will freeze the tears

you cry before they fall. your eyes will lie

to you in white. listen, your body is tunneling

holes through an avalanche. your body

is hiding itself inside someone you have

never met. your coat is the translucent duffel bag

in which the universe carries all its weights.

on this planet the sun shines blue. we wear igloos

on our heads as hats. no one will want to visit

you here. we say, *this world, this wait, this longest year.*

WHAT IS A FOREST IF NOT EVERY LOUD THING ECHOED

every broken branch a death
    of something dear. feet smack
against ground like gunshots.
    this is the way the deer falls,
the woman slumps, the car fails
    when hit by the slug. and miss.
and dark. a reflection in the ice
    shows snow falling at night,
your sweetest dog seizing on
    the steps before the house,
your first love seizing in a car
    by a pond. and all of this
again, rewound, snapped back,
    a spine broke. this is the fault
of water, and sound, and lack.
    a tree fell and nobody
heard it. your skull cracked on
    impact. and what's left—a muffled
echo, rust flaked on clean snow?

GRIEF AS ART APPRECIATION

right now I am inches
    from a memory, trying to spot
        intricacies in its grain

& I pray at night to no god
    only to shrink & be spread across
        the lightless rivers that move among matter

POEM IN WHICH I AM TRAPPED IN A THOUSAND SNOWY VALLEYS

& everywhere I look is up | endless dead wood to climb to nowhere | tracks without animals, a crunch of leaves I can't see | here is where somebody left oversized footprints in the snow | I follow his steps exactly, & trip | this ground a long prickle-branched hush | skinned knees leave rosy smears on white | my dog is dying in the hills | her panting is a plaintive sound, echoed down | I am a thousand-pound steel chest cavity I am can't leave I am stuck foot sunk in ice in a creek | cars speed through the mountains on roads I won't reach | everyone is driving away | there is nothing near but the sound of dying, the stink of her breath, the snow | and a thousand stories all end the same | my ankle snaps | she pants | I'm too late | she stops, alone

V

WHAT IS A TRAVELER IF NOT EVERY STRANGE THING

to you who have lived on lava fields:
what do you make of blood? this earth
leaves a thousand traces, and still

it has no family. millions of other planets
might exist where humans could survive, but

they are all eons out of reach. we are only alone
if we number the miles. if I traveled eight

hundred trillion light-years I bet I'd find
the place the dead live. if I stole a strong enough
telescope I know I'd touch their hands again.

I WAKE IN AN OLD FACTORY

curled up on a bed of bent screws, ceiling above
cavernous as the sky. I vaulted myself in last
night through a shattered window—all fine-edged
glass and splinters. my knees hit the ground
with a sharp scrape of blood. no one waited outside

because he didn't want to get caught. the wall
between us spoke miles. *come
inside*, I said, running a hand along a rusted

piece of machinery. it left orange flakes on my palm.
I blew them off like wishes. *I think I see someone*,
he called. his nervousness washed over
the room like the soapy wet stick of a popped
bubble. to escape I climbed to the peak

of a rickety tower of discarded tin. from it I could
see for lifetimes. my hair blew back in no wind. *I am
the only living thing in this system*, I said

aloud to no one. I told the empty space where
he might still be standing—*I left the outside
years ago*. my voice arrived an echo, singed
my tongue like a lost queen's quiet hiss.
I was just a witness. nothing more, nothing less.

IF I WERE A SPEEDING TRAIN (A CYBORG LOVE SONG)

in a field of bluebonnets I am winding—
a clock, my past—I am blue, wearing a bonnet.

or I am the sky: composed of loose parts. I cannot
hold me anymore. how much of us can be

replaced with iron—a kneecap, a hip, a heart?

let us fit ourselves with gears.
let us wheel ourselves nearer.

if I could I would cart you across
oceans, tucked away as precious cargo

in my robot chest. but I have no door,
no key, no bloodless steel cavity. no—

I'll never be this speeding train: the long stitch
across the belly of the country,

the struck pendulum, the prison.

O HELL O HELL THAT MILD THING

once, I thought
if you were a reed I would play you
with my teeth.
the mouth on you.
I thought
o red ship

and ignored the way
it was always sinking

WHAT THIS LACKS IS UNDERSTANDING

say, a thorn in the side of the letter *r*, or the lumbering way an unpracticed language sounds as it stumbles past fat clumsy lips. there is an element of reckless unfocus in the way new words move: a blank dumbness, like the white noise on the radio from a station that faded miles ago but

remains unchanged. to the moose on the edge of a road somewhere: might I have antlers too? if I did I would spear a thorn or *þrjú*. every *eth* would roll easy off my tongue. it would not taste thick with spit and old smoke and waking up. somebody says not this lisp of dream again. not an ash-cloud of sky not a blurry patch of painted plaster

to peel from the walls, from the bone—but what's it mean to strike a beast with a car, to see the metal and flesh collide into some new-age hybrid monster, what's it mean when for a moment you wish it would absorb the impact seek revenge and break down the walls of the house up the road where your parents lived or live or sit watching the clock and waiting for you, and what might you do if it did? if it unstuck all these thorns from your chipped teeth and took the words you can't shape and tore them into pieces, little strips of confetti

and unkempt hate? the work of language is how it lies in translation. what this lacks is *þýðir*, or perhaps *a sense of purpose*. the sad truth is the moose lived and you lived and you made it to the house and nobody cared, and nothing changed. and nothing ended. but all poems are about death, somebody said. the struck moose with the graveled fur, maybe, or the flies that flocked to the swash of skin and matted hair left smeared across the asphalt—

ON ESCAPING BLACK HOLES

I say that black hole there tastes just like
delight. a dark sweet weight, marrowjuiced bones.

the goal is to turn back before getting ripped
into infinite strips, like spaghetti—unlike my

grandfather, who died coughing up strings
of his own organs, bloody gray-pink tissue.

we explore what we swallow.
I mean, we are swallowed by the things

we explore—cigarettes and
deep space and chemicals and all of this

is to say you are headed for collapse.
a star, a planet, your heart, your brain.

a singularity is both a black hole and the big bang.

and how do you want to die?
in an inferno; *in my lungs*; *in sleep*;

in the sky. this world is dull and dusty
and I am hacking slowly down. look,

I've killed before. if I press my forehead
to the body of the star it'll freeze this fever out.

is the sound I hear an engine? is it my bones
stretching by? I always heard time

might run backward inside.
we have done this all before, and died.

A FEW THINGS THAT HAUNT ME

the electrons in your atoms & the atoms
    in your cells & the cells
        in your bones & what it all
            becomes & where it all goes

HERE THE CLOUDS ARE WOOL BLANKETS

they are piles from shorn sheep.
        I've never found god in the sunset

before, or now. I've never found.
        when I left New York the haze hit

the eye of the earth. when I left
        New York I left footprints

on the old brick face of his building.
        here I am walking sideways

down first avenue. he hung
        a ceramic duck outside so I would

always know where he was.
        he hung it from my collarbone,

see how it swings between my lungs?
        they say mine is a beggar's prayer.

I found god on a subway platform.
        I didn't. I got lost

in the Bronx and all my trains
        were out. vomit on the ground.

the rattle a dusky bright sound. here
        is the eye again, this time

through the frost of an airplane
        window. a seatmate's flank flops

past the armrest, floral-print cotton
        damp against my elbow.

I think there must be safety in wool: thick,
        a clothed set. I found god in

the way zero becomes
        a whole. I mean, I found no god

in a collection of zero sum equations.
        the clouds can be blankets

if you don't need to touch them.
        or, a blanket can be cold and wet.

a clammy floral shirt can be as good
        a god as any. I pretend

but the truth is I've never known
        how to find my way alone.

LAMBDA MEANS GOD IF YOU'RE SEARCHING FOR ONE

you might say fish are uncoordinated in flight. not waves—unless we find waves in air. if you were a particle, a moment, a sound, alight. you are reaching for a syllable, falling. you are still underwater. untethered or unsinkable. we are all made of porous skin, but nobody knows how to drown and get away with it. there is something to be said, but not in words, or worlds—but there is something here. a world made of Os, round mouthfeel. some talk of dinosaurs might calm that screaming child. were he in water would he be comfortable? only warm— a womb, a prison, a sentence. or not. some talk of physics might put him right to sleep. lambda weights an equation but no one knows what it means. sheep jump over planets, we count them one-by-one. there is a smoothed-out circle somewhere. nowhere. a smoothed-out universe. a planet lacking corners. see: playschool or soft plastic. here we come back to dinosaurs: syrupy remnants of feathered things. and here we come back to liquid. we will become something malleable. after an age we will span miles of empty land, and grow wider all the while. grow wilder. and encompassing—see? the body always knows itself. the mouth stretches across time, forever finds itself a larger, more perfect O—

TERRAFORM

i.
the cobweb in the corner of the ceiling
vibrates with the sound of it: all planets & noise,

this music set to the universe's static—the grandest
case of tinnitus doctors never diagnosed.

the spider eats a fly, wrapped.
I pick at the skin around my fingernails.

ii.

my ex-lover told me that one night on the porch
he heard three cockroaches mating   & he saw it
as it happened, & the noise was
               this slight, moist, exoskeletal rubbing—

like a tiny washboard   in a tiny bluegrass band
like the predator
          shrunk & slowed down to a crawl

& the finish was something profoundly   unsettling
    the shuddering
       close of wing.   the dismount

the flushed, satisfied scurry
                     across bare feet

iii.

maybe all living things

vibrate   at this same frequency

maybe we time   our breaths & thrusts & chirps

to mete a harmony with unseen   moons

       with the gone stars we're made of—

iv.

now the web is tensed & still; now
                the spider lounges, bloated

now   I am heavy
      a gas giant   now   I rise
            become   a crumb   in no atmosphere

v.

maybe we are so small   so unbreathing

maybe we make no sounds
        to the universe at all—

vi.
skin terraformed, I am
      transformed

into some new earth ripe for alien life

   I tell this to the universe   & wait
        & wait

I tell this to the universe
      & it says nothing back

POEM IN WHICH I AM DRIVING TOWARD A HOME

someone once told me all planets but this one
are named after gods. it is not enough just to know

such things exist. & this life such a short road. & your body
a long-lost shape. a wind tunnel, collapsed siding—
will you be forever nowhere? I glimpse the outline of your lungs

in mountain mist. you meteor shower, you wild
uncertain dark! I can't stand the flat of you. I am speaking

from inside a mouth that is itself an overflow
of legs, a pair of lips brushed with black
exoskeletal crust. here words are beetles, they breed

between my teeth. your name a dense protein
on my tongue & still too small to contain

the whole of you. did you know it's only recent history
since humans crawled from the muck & began
to grow hands? you unformed vanished self, you clipped

disembodied wish. even in absence, I've never stopped naming
you. what I am trying to say is *I am almost there, I am coming*

soon. to ask—*where are you.* have I ever even touched
your skin? I must have scorched you in my leaving,
I've heard talk of years of drought. & me in this wet.

me in this insect mouth. this trip has lasted
all too long. listen, I am just now trying to arrive.

NOTES

A caveat to these notes: I am neither a scientist nor a mathematician—only an enthusiast. I understand just enough of the various concepts I used in these poems to riff off them creatively. But for anyone who is interested, these are some of the ideas that have captured my attention and awe over the years, and sparked the inspiration for several of the poems in this collection.

dark matter: Twenty-five percent of our universe is made up of dark matter, which is matter that does not absorb, reflect, or emit light, or interact in any way with the electromagnetic force. We can't see it, but we know that it's there because it has a gravitational effect on visible matter. One fun, relatively understandable intro-to-dark-matter resource is the "Scotohylology" episode of the Ologies podcast (interview with particle physicist Dr. Flip Tanedo), released February 8, 2023.

"astronomers capture violent newborn star": This title comes from a Space.com RSS feed from May 26, 2014, which linked to a Hubble and NASA press release titled "Violent birth announcement from an infant star." The star in question is IRAS 14568-6304, located in the Circinus molecular cloud. This poem is riffing off the fact that we can't ever truly come into contact with anything else, at an atomic level. What our brains register as touch is actually the electrons in our atoms repelling the electrons surrounding the atoms of whatever we think we're touching. This means we're always separated—by a microscopic distance, but a distance nonetheless—from everything else in the universe.

there is a world in which soup doesn't film: Some multiverse theories posit that a new universe springs up every single time a choice is made, anywhere in any universe. Some of these worlds might be close to ours—maybe even like this world that I wish I lived in—but the vast majority would likely be so detached from our current reality that we couldn't even use human language to describe them. Several poems in this collection are interested in the idea of multiverses.

Askja: In 1965 and 1967, nine of the twelve astronauts who would later set foot on the moon trained for their missions in the Askja caldera in Iceland, a location chosen due to its geological similarity to the moon.

when the mara *weights my chest I see*: The *mara* (Old Norse, meaning "nightmare") is a malicious being in Northern European folklore who rides on the chest of sleeping people and brings them nightmares.

this mimicked dance: The fastest manmade object is currently the NASA Parker Solar Probe, which launched in 2018 and has reached a speed of 532,000 kilometers per hour (kph) using the sun's gravity. By 2025 it will travel as fast as 690,000 kph . . . which is still only 0.064 percent of the speed of light.

drinking on the porch with a fellow recluse: This poem is after Li Po's poem, "Drinking in the Mountains with a Recluse," as translated by David Hinton in *The New Directions Anthology of Classical Chinese Poetry*.

theories of relativity: The theory of relativity is composed of two interrelated theories, that of general relativity and special relativity. General relativity has to do with gravitation, special relativity with the absence of it. The consequences of general relativity that are relevant to this poem are that clocks move more slowly in deeper gravitational wells (i.e., places of higher gravity, like planets) and that both spacetime and light rays bend in the presence of a gravitational field. So the amount that the universe and the light curves around various objects depends on how massive they are.

we call man an insect infinite: What would happen to you if you were caught in the vacuum of space without a spacesuit? First, atmospheric pressure determines the temperatures at which liquids boil; this is why water boils faster on a mountaintop than at sea level. In space, there's no atmospheric pressure, and our bodies are 60 percent water. With no pressure, that liquid would boil immediately, so as the water turned to gas all your body tissues would begin to expand. The vacuum of space would also pull all the air out of your lungs, and then pull out gas and water vapor once you had no air left. Then you would freeze, first your nose and mouth and then the rest of you.

poem in which acid rain is just acid: This poem (and many others throughout this collection) plays with the idea that naming an indefinite pronoun (everything, everyone, somebody, etc.) or a negation (nothing, no one, nobody, neither, etc.) invariably makes it something—a referent with some specific meaning—rather than the nonexistence of meaning or understanding. I view these as fun linguistic versions of the old woman/young woman optical illusions.

safe travels: This poem references the song "Safe Travels (Don't Die)" by Lisa Hannigan.

escapism as a quantum thought experiment: This poem plays with the ideas behind the Schrödinger's cat paradox, which imagines an experiment where a cat is trapped in a box with poison that will be released if a radioactive atom decays. Because radioactivity is a quantum process and is thus subject to quantum superposition, before the box is opened the atom has both decayed and not decayed, and the cat is both alive and dead. It only resolves into one event when it has been observed (this is known as the measurement problem).

language in which slabb *is the worst kind of snow*: *Slabb* is the word for partially melted snow mixed with rainwater. It technically means nothing—it's an onomatopoeia for the sound it makes when you're walking through it.

what is a traveler if not every strange thing: Technically, there's only one planet where humans can survive, and it's the one we live on. But theoretically—there are trillions of planets in our galaxy, and probably somewhere in the range of 10 septillion planets in the larger universe. NASA's Kepler mission monitored 100,000 stars over four years and observed more than 900 Earth-sized planets; 23 of those planets are in the habitable zone. Scientists did various analyses and found that on average, 30 percent of stars have at least one Earth-sized, temperate planet. Extrapolating, that would be 90 billion Earth-sized, temperate planets in our galaxy alone. This doesn't mean we could survive on all of them, or any of them. It's almost certainly impossible. But . . . we dream.

on escaping black holes: A singularity is a point or region of infinite mass density at which space and time are infinitely distorted by gravitational forces (i.e., where spacetime entirely collapses). Black holes are the most well-known singularities, and we still don't know what happens inside of them. Gravity is so intense in a black hole that it sucks everything nearby into it—think of a sheet suspended in the air, corners pulled tight so it's straight and mostly flat across, with some little toys or marbles scattered across it. Now put a heavy rock in the middle of that sheet. If this were the universe, and this were the kind of black hole that causes spaghettification, all the toys and marbles rolling toward the center would be stretched into long, thin strips as they approached the heavy rock.

here the clouds are wool blankets: This is loosely inspired by the fact that all infinite processes exist around the concept of zero. In mathematics, zero is called the empty set, and it is always a closed set (i.e., it contains all its limits). Zero to infinity is also a closed set. Most important things given to us by mathematics wouldn't exist without zero: algebra, calculus, electronics, computers, etc. Zero is my favorite number, simultaneously abstraction and reality. I can never wrap my head around it. See Robert Kaplan's book, *The Nothing That Is: A Natural History of Zero*, to learn more about zero than I could ever attempt to explain. The poem also references the song "Beggar's Prayer" by Emiliana Torrini.

lambda means god if you're searching for one: In 1917, Einstein predicted the existence of dark energy with what became known as the cosmological constant, represented by lambda. Physicists still have no clear idea what dark energy is; we know that it makes up approximately 70 percent of the universe, and is the mysterious repulsive force that drives the universe's accelerated expansion. (As mentioned earlier, dark matter makes up 25 percent of the universe, and then a measly 5 percent is all the matter and light we can experience and see.)

terraform: This poem was inspired by *The Space Project*, a Record Store Day compilation album released in 2014 that took recordings made by the Voyager I and II spacecrafts in the 1970s and gave them to a variety of bands to create songs around.

poem in which I am driving toward a home: The first line of this poem is a reference to the poem "The Body Deformed by Tidal Forces" by Lillian-Yvonne Bertram.

ACKNOWLEDGMENTS

Many thanks to the journals in which versions of these poems previously appeared:

The Adroit Journal: "dark matter" and "no vacancy"
The Boiler Journal: "elegy for all the times we used to get drunk," "feeling ill in a novelty restaurant," and "if I were a speeding train (a cyborg love song)"
Fugue: "o hell o hell that mild thing"
The Journal: "poem in which I am leaning against a car"
New Delta Review: "what this lacks is understanding"
The Pinch Journal: "on escaping black holes," "poem in which I drive drunk," and "the moral of the story is *bears aren't friends*"
Poetry Northwest: "language in which *slabb* is the worst kind of snow" and "family reunion (the Norsemen return)"
Portland Review: "we call man an insect infinite" and "poem in which the sun is a balding and jealous lover"
Smoking Glue Gun: "when the *mara* weights my chest I see" and "there is a world in which the big dipper is the freckles on my arm"
Spork: "poem in which acid rain is just acid"
Terrain.org: "armistice," "astronomers capture violent newborn star," and "terraform"

A thousand thank yous to KMA Sullivan and the team at YesYes. A first book is special. Thank you for giving it your care and attention, and for helping me make it real.

Thank you to my family, and especially to Jeannine and Bill Prince, JJ Prince, Mike Prince, Forrest Durey, Stan Durey, and Erin Johnson, for your support, inspiration, and influence on the poems in this book. Thank you for letting me write about you and the people close to you.

Thanks to the many friends, teachers, and ever-loving companion-animals who have supported me, inspired me, or helped me over the ten years I spent working on the poems in this book: Ana Alvarez, Sarah Andrew, Kristen Bickerstaff, Samantha Deal, Becky Eades, Devyn Howery, Kathleen Jones, Laurel Jones, Margot Kahn Case, Mark Kelly, Veronica Lupinacci, Chris Nymeyer, and Cathe Shubert; Evie Atom Atkinson, Lillian-Yvonne Bertram, Wendy Brenner, Zachary Harris, A. Van Jordan, Sarah Messer, Ben Pelhan, Anne Marie Rooney, S. E. Smith, Beth Staples, and Michael White; Bailey, Daisy, and Cassidy.

Special thank yous to Malena Mörling, for your guidance and wisdom; to John Okrent, for helping me find the key; and to Aleah Chapin, first for your friendship, and second for letting us use your gorgeous and unsettling art on the cover of this book.

Thank you most of all to Gabe Moseley, for your love and your support and your unwavering belief in me.

KATIE PRINCE is a poet and essayist. Her first poetry book, *Tell This to the Universe*, was a finalist for the 2019 National Poetry Series and won the 2021 Pamet River Prize from YesYes Books. In the spring of 2017, she served as artist-in-residence at Klaustrið, in Iceland's Fljótsdalur valley, and in 2019, she received a GAP Award from Artist Trust to continue working on the project she began there. She holds an MFA in poetry from the University of North Carolina, Wilmington. Her work has been published in *Electric Literature*, *New South*, *Fugue*, the *Adroit Journal*, and *Poetry Northwest*, among others. You can find her online at www.katieprince.com.

ALSO FROM YESYES BOOKS

FICTION
Girls Like Me by Nina Packebush
Three Queerdos and a Baby by Nina Packebush

WRITING RESOURCES
Gathering Voices: Creating a Community-Based Poetry Workshop by Marty McConnell

FULL-LENGTH COLLECTIONS
Ugly Music by Diannely Antigua
Bone Language by Jamaica Baldwin
Cataloguing Pain by Allison Blevins
What Runs Over by Kayleb Rae Candrilli
This, Sisyphus by Brandon Courtney
40 WEEKS by Julia Kolchinsky Dasbach
Salt Body Shimmer by Aricka Foreman
Gutter by Lauren Brazeal Garza
Forever War by Kate Gaskin
Inconsolable Objects by Nancy Miller Gomez
Ceremony of Sand by Rodney Gomez
Undoll by Tanya Grae
Loudest When Startled by luna rey hall
Everything Breaking / For Good by Matt Hart
Sons of Achilles by Nabila Lovelace
Otherlight by Jill Mceldowney
Landscape with Sex and Violence by Lynn Melnick
Refusenik by Lynn Melnick
GOOD MORNING AMERICA I AM HUNGRY AND ON FIRE by jamie mortara
Born Backwards by Tanya Olson
Stay by Tanya Olson

a falling knife has no handle by Emily O'Neill
To Love An Island by Ana Portnoy Brimmer
Another Way to Split Water by Alycia Pirmohamed
One God at a Time by Meghan Privitello
I'm So Fine: A List of Famous Men & What I Had On by Khadijah Queen
If the Future Is a Fetish by Sarah Sgro
Gilt by Raena Shirali
Say It Hurts by Lisa Summe
Boat Burned by Kelly Grace Thomas
Helen Or My Hunger by Gale Marie Thompson
As She Appears by Shelley Wong

RECENT CHAPBOOK COLLECTIONS

Vinyl 45s
    Inside My Electric City by Caylin Capra-Thomas
    Exit Pastoral by Aidan Forster
    Crown for the Girl Inside by Lisa Low
    Of Darkness and Tumbling by Mónica Gomery
    Juned by Jenn Marie Nunes
    Scavenger by Jessica Lynn Suchon
    Unmonstrous by John Allen Taylor
    Preparing the Body by Norma Liliana Valdez
    Giantess by Emily Vizzo

Blue Note Editions
    Kissing Caskets by Mahogany L. Browne
    One Above One Below: Positions & Lamentations by Gala Mukomolova
    The Porch (As Sanctuary) by Jae Nichelle